Bargain
April 20(

Reduced

THE HEYDAY OF THE TRAM - 2

PETER WALLER

IAN ALLAN Publishing

Introduction

First published 1996

ISBN 0 7110 23964

Designed by Alan C. Butcher

Published by Ian Allan Publishing

an imprint of Ian Allan Ltd, Terminal House, Station Approach, Shepperton, Surrey TW17 8AS.
Printed by Ian Allan Printing Ltd, Coombelands House, Coombelands Lane, Addlestone, Weybridge, Surrey KT15 1HY.

In 1992 Ian Allan Ltd published *The Heyday of the Tram*. Although there were those that criticised the use of the word 'Heyday', the book was well-received and certainly generated many favourable comments. Whilst the number of people taking transparencies of trams from the early 1950s onwards were relatively few, it has proved possible to gather together a second selection which, it is hoped, will be of equal interest. Inevitably, it has not proved possible to find illustrations for all the tramways that existed into the postwar years, although the majority of the major systems are represented to some extent.

In the 50 years since the end of World War 2 the wheel of public transport has turned almost full circle. In the immediate postwar years electric street transport was perceived as being a contributory factor to traffic congestion — as, given the general lack of segregation, it probably was — and the greater flexibility that the diesel bus and, to a lesser extent, the trolleybus offered was important in the reconstruction and growth of urban areas after 1945. Few who have seen the classic documentary *The elephant will never forget* can themselves forget the scene at the end of the film when Lord Latham, then Chairman of the London Transport Executive, welcomed the final tram back to its depart with the immortal words 'Goodbye *old* tram'. In 1952 it did seem that the tramcar was on its way out as a means of transport as, gradually, all the great tramway bastions fell to the all-conquering bus — London in 1952, Birmingham in 1953, Belfast in 1954, Dundee and Edinburgh in 1956, Liverpool in 1957, Aberdeen in 1958, Leeds in 1959, Sheffield in 1960 and, last but by no means least, Glasgow in 1962. Even smaller towns, such as Gateshead and Sunderland, where the tram had retained a pivotal role in public transport provision, succumbed in the decade or so after peace.

There were odd places that stuck out against the fashion — Blackpool (although losing its 'town' routes), Great Orme and the Isle of Man — but as a means of mass urban public transport, its primary function, the tram, to all intents and purposes, disappeared in Britain with the final Glasgow closures. But the pundits were to be wrong when they wrote the tram off. Traffic congestion did not miraculously disappear from the streets once the tram track had been lifted; if anything, with the constant growth in the numbers of both private cars and commercial vehicles, the problem has got worse. Moreover, the realisation has come that the internal combustion engine, whilst offering a great deal of personal freedom to the individual, has a down side in terms of the pollution caused and, amidst increasing scares about the quality of air in urban areas, thoughts are turning once again to improved public transport — at the heart of which the tram, or Light Rail Vehicle, is witnessing a considerable revival.

Although two earlier schemes — the Tyne & Wear Metro and the Docklands Light Railway — have both proved remarkably successful, neither can be regarded as tramways in the conventional sense. The Tyne & Wear Metro, based around the old British Rail suburban electrified lines in the Newcastle area, is more heavy than light rail, whilst the Docklands Light Railway is only now really starting to fulfil its true potential. Extensions into the city and to Beckton, the construction of a replacement fleet of vehicles and the probability that it will be extended south of the river, means that the DLR is finally providing the public transport so desperately needed for the regeneration of the docklands area. But neither the Metro nor the DLR included any traditional street tramway; for the first stretch of urban street tramway to be opened in Britain for almost two generations we have to look to the Manchester Metrolink.

This pioneering system, the first of the second generation electric tramways, owes its birth to an accident of railway history — the fact that the two major surviving main line stations in Manchester were separate. Proposals for a link line, including the ill-fated Picc-Vic underground, came to nought, and the horde of minibuses that provided a useful connection merely added to the urban congestion. The radical decision to build a Light Rail between the two, connecting into (and replacing) the existing BR lines to Bury and Altrincham emerged in the 1980s. With its phased opening in 1992 Britain could at last claim a Light Rail system comparable to operations in many of the major European cities.

Since the Manchester opening, the Sheffield Supertram has also been opened and further progress has been made on other projects, most notably the Croydon Tramlink and the Midlands Metro. By the end of the century, ironically almost exactly 100 years after the first boom in electric tramways in Britain, second generation trams could be operating in many of the country's towns and cities. We are, in all probability, arriving at the Millenium at the dawn of a new heyday of the tram.

I hope that this look back to the past and preview of the future will bring back memories for those who remember the tramways that we have lost and for those, like myself, for whom the real heyday is yet to come, a colourful memorial to what we have missed.

Peter Waller
August 1995

Acknowledgements
I would like to thank the following for allowing me access to their photographic collections: Roy Brook, C. Carter, Paul Collins, Peter Durham, Geoff Lumb, Tom Marsh, Brian Morrison and Ron White (Colour-Rail). Without their help it would have proved impossible to compile this selection. The number of people taking tram photographs in colour during the 1950s and 1960s were few and we must be grateful for the foresight of those that did. Without their efforts three or four decades ago, we would not have the ability to create this trip into the past.

Glasgow

Title page: 'Coronation' No 1220 heads northwestwards towards Maryhill on route 29 from Tollcross. This tram, new in November 1938, was rebodied in 1942 after being destroyed by fire in February the same year. It was to survive in service for a further 20 years. Route 29 was converted to bus operation on 21 October 1961. A number of 'Coronations' survive in preservation: No 1173 at the Glasgow Museum of Transport, No 1245 at Carlton Colville, No 1274 in the United States and No 1282 at the National Tramway Museum. *Geoff Lumb*

Aberdeen

Left: Originally built in 1923 in the Corporation's own workshops, No 99 dated from 1923. Built as an open vestibule car on a Brill 21E truck, the car was later fully enclosed and fitted with a Peckham P35 truck. The car is seen at the Woodside terminus in August 1955. By this date the Woodside route had only a few months left to operate, being converted to bus operation on 26 November 1955. The tram was to last slightly longer, being withdrawn in 1956. *Roy Brook*

4

Left:
A line-up of hospital specials is seen on the Woodend spur in August 1954 headed by No 137. This Brush-built car, the last of a batch of 12 delivered in 1929, was fully-enclosed from new and was fitted with a P35 truck. These trams were withdrawn between 1955 and 1958. The Woodend spur was situated on the Hazlehead route. The two-mile stretch, from Rubislaw to Hazlehead including the Woodend spur, opened on 16 July 1926 and replaced a bus service that had been introduced five years earlier to serve a new housing estate. The Hazlehead route was converted to bus operation on 7 October 1956. *Roy Brook*

Above:
In the immediate post-World War 2 years Aberdeen was one of the few British tram systems from which there were positive signs. It was widely believed that the Sea Beach route, construction of which had been suspended as a result of the war, would be completed and a batch of 20 streamlined cars, Nos 19-38, was delivered in 1949. Built by Pickering and fitted with EMB bogies, these were, however, to be the last new trams delivered to Aberdeen. No 24 is pictured at Bridge of Dee, the southern terminus of the main route that ran northwards to Bridge of Don. This was destined to be the last Aberdeen route to succumb to the all-conquering diesel bus, being replaced on 3 May 1958. Sister car No 36 had the dubious distinction of being Aberdeen's last car; it is to be regretted that none of these stylish cars survived into preservation. *Roy Brook*

5

Belfast

Left:
Constructed to the unusual gauge of 4ft 9in, the city of Belfast had an extensive tramway network that gradually succumbed to the trolleybus and diesel bus from 1936 onwards. Although in rapid decline by the early 1950s, it was still possible to see many trams in operation, particularly at peak periods. Here there is a line up of four 'McCreary' cars and one 'Chamberlain' on Queen's Road in August 1953. The 50 'Chamberlain' cars were built in 1930, with 40 being constructed by Brush and the remainder by the locally-based Service Motor Works company. *Roy Brook*

Right:
One of the Brush-built 'Chamberlain' cars, No 364, is pictured in Donegall Square North in September 1953. By this date the Belfast network had shrunk considerably, with the only routes surviving being the two to Ligoniel, via Crumlin Road and via Shankill Road, and that to Queens Road. The 'Chamberlain' cars, which outlasted the newer 'McCreary' cars, were fitted with Maley & Taunton 8ft 0in swinglink trucks.
W. E. Robertson/Colour-Rail (IR342)

'McCreary' car No 409 is seen in College Square East during August 1953 with a service to Ligoniel. By this date the decline of the Belfast system was rapid; all-day operation over the surviving routes ceased two months later, on 10/11 October, although rush-hour services continued to operate until February the following year. The last scheduled services were operated on 10 February 1954 and the official closure occurred on 28 February. The 50 'McCreary' cars were the last new trams delivered to Belfast. Built in 1935/36, 20 (Nos 392, 423-441) were built by English Electric and the remainder (Nos 393-422) by Service Motor Works. Although the 'McCreary' cars represented the most modern cars in the fleet, all were withdrawn before the final closure and the last cars to operate were the old 'Chamberlain' type. None of the 'McCreary' cars survives, although 'Chamberlain' No 357 is preserved in Northern Ireland. *Roy Brook*

Birmingham

Right:
Car No 420, one of a batch of 50 built by the United Electric Car Co in 1912, is pictured outbound on the Alcester Lanes End route. This route was converted to bus operation on 2 October 1949 along with the other Moseley services. All the trams in this particular batch, with one exception, survived World War 2, but they were to be withdrawn between 1947 and 1949 as Birmingham's postwar tram conversion programme took effect. *C. Carter*

Left:
Cars Nos 737, of 1926/27, and 532, of 1913, stand at the terminus of the Rubery route, No 71, in 1949. No 532 was delivered in 1913 and, like No 420, was built by UEC as a open-balcony car. It was one of a batch of 75 that were fitted with enclosed balconies between 1926 and 1931. No 737, a product of Brush, was delivered as a fully-enclosed car. It was one of a batch of 30 constructed in 1926/27 that were fitted with EMB 'Burnley' type bogies. These cars were the first to be fitted for operation in Birmingham with air brakes from new. The Rubery route, along with the remainder of the Bristol Road services, was converted to bus operation on 6 July 1952. *C. Carter*

The city centre terminus for the routes out along the Bristol and Moseley Roads, amongst others, was Navigation Street. Pictured shortly before the route's conversion, on 2 October 1949, to bus operation, Brush-built car No 730 is seen on route No 37 to Cannon Hill. The final closure of the Birmingham system was to occur on 4 July 1953 when the Short Heath, Pype Hayes and Erdington routes were converted to bus operation. With Birmingham's demise, the once extensive 3ft 6in gauge network in the West Midlands had disappeared. *C. Carter*

Blackpool

The last traditional double-deck trams to operate in Britain were the few Blackpool 'Standards' that survived until final withdrawal in 1966. The story of the 'Standards', however, dates back to the rebuilding of five of the 'Marton Box' cars between 1918 and 1923. From these were developed the 'Standards', the first of which, No 43, appeared (as a nominal rebuild of the similarly numbered 'Motherwell' car of 1902) in 1923. Over the next six years some 40 of the type were to emerge, all of which, with the exception of seven (Nos 146-152), were built in Blackpool's own workshops at Rigby Road. The first withdrawals occurred in 1940, but many survived into the 1950s, despite the introduction of the streamlined cars, and eight survived into the next decade. Two of the type, including No 48 on the left (which is now preserved in Oregon, USA, after withdrawal in 1962), are seen in Gynn Square in 1955. *Roy Brook*

In 1928 English Electric built 10 cars, Nos 167-176, which were initially fitted with pantographs for use on the Fleetwood route. Known as either 'Pantograph' or 'Pullman' cars, the pantographs were replaced with conventional trolley poles in 1933. No 175 is seen outside Blackpool North station prior to departure northwards with a service to Fleetwood. Between 1950 and 1953 Nos 168-175 received English Electric replacement bogies, which had been released due to the modernisation of Nos 10-21. All the 'Pantograph' cars were withdrawn by 1961, although a number were used as the basis for some of the illuminated trams for which Blackpool is rightly famous. No 167 is preserved at the National Tramway Museum. No 175 was not so lucky, however; it was scrapped in 1963. *Tom Marsh*

During the 1930s, under the inspired management of Walter Luff, the Blackpool system was to receive more than 100 modern streamlined trams. These cars were to form the basis of the Blackpool fleet for more than 60 years and many remain in service.

No 214, seen at Little Bispham on 22 May 1960, was one of a batch of English Electric cars delivered in 1934. These cars were withdrawn during the period from 1961 until 1965 during the period when the Blackpool tram network shrank back to the coastal route

from Fleetwood to Starr Gate with the closure of the remaining town routes. *Geoff Lumb*

Left:
A second type of streamlined car, and one well-suited to the holiday traffic that formed so much a part of Blackpool's summer trade, was the 'Boat'. A total of 12 of the type were built by English Electric and a number remain in service. No 230, later renumbered 600 and still owned by Blackpool Transport albeit on long-term loan to the Heaton Park Tramway, is seen at Bispham on 22 May 1960. *Geoff Lumb*

SEE ALSO PAGE 74.

Above:
The 1930s also saw the delivery of two batches of streamlined double-deckers. Thirteen, Nos 237-249, were constructed as open-toppers and known as 'Luxury Dreadnoughts', whilst a further 14, Nos 250-263 were delivered as fully-enclosed cars. The 'Luxury Dreadnoughts' were later to be fully enclosed. All survived to be renumbered in the sequence 700-726 in 1968 and the majority remain in service more than 60 years after they were built. No 723, originally numbered 260, is pictured entering the Pleasure Beach loop. *Michael H. Waller*

The final flowering of the Luff modernisation plan came with the delivery of 25 single-deck cars in 1953, Nos 304-328. Known, inevitably, as the 'Coronation' class, the Charles Roberts-built trams were, unfortunately, not as successful as the earlier streamlined cars and withdrawals commenced in 1963. A number were modified, but this did not lead to the same sort of longevity as the 1930s-built cars. The last was withdrawn in 1975 although one remains in the Blackpool fleet for use on specials; two others have also been preserved. Two of the type are seen at North Pier shortly after their introduction into service; note the Union Flag motif on the trolley base of the car nearest the camera.
Roy Brook

Blackpool & Fleetwood

The route of the surviving coastal tramway north from North station to Fleetwood was originally operated by the Blackpool & Fleetwood Tramroad Co. The line opened in 1898 and was taken over by Blackpool Corporation on 1 January 1920. The company took delivery of 10 toastrack trams, Nos 1-10, from G. F. Milnes & Co in 1898 and these survived in service until the 1930s.

On withdrawal a number were converted into works' cars and, in 1960, the last survivor, No 2, was restored for use in the 75th anniversary celebrations of Blackpool's electric tramway. It is seen here as restored at Rigby Road depot on 22 May 1960. The car is now preserved as part of the National Tramway Museum's collection. *Geoff Lumb*

Another ex-Blackpool & Fleetwood Tramroad Co car restored for the 1960 celebrations was enclosed single-decker No 40, which originally dated from 1914. The car, seen here at Rigby Road depot on 15 October 1960, was repainted in the old chestnut-brown and white livery of the company. Both it and No 2 were presented to the Tramway Museum Society in 1962, and No 40 can now be seen on display at the Heaton Park Tramway in Manchester.
Roy Brook

Bolton

Although no Bolton trams were preserved when the system was finally converted to bus operation in 1947, one car, No 66, was subsequently rescued and has been fully restored. Based for almost 15 years in Blackpool, the 1901-built veteran is seen in Rigby Road depot on 18 July 1981 in the company of overhead repair car No 754. This tram also dated originally from 1901 and was one of the 'Marton Box' cars that predated Blackpool's famous 'Standards'. It was converted to an overhead repair car in 1934 and remained in service until 1982. On withdrawal it was preserved at the North of England Open Air Museum at Beamish and has now been fully restored to its original condition as Blackpool No 31.
Michael H. Waller

Bradford

On 6 May 1950, buses replaced trams of the last section of the Bradford tram network — the Horsfall Playing Fields route — and with Bradford's demise came the end of the 4ft 0in gauge tram in Britain. This was not, however, to be the end of tramway operation in Bradford, as the last car, No 104, was to find a temporary home as a scoreboard at the city's Odsal stadium. It was rescued from there three years later and, after a period of careful restoration, was to be operated again over the tram track that had survived at Thornbury depot for the first time since withdrawal on 23 July 1958. The tram continued to make occasional appearances, as here on 7 May 1960, until the early 1960s. After a period of storage, No 104, which was Bradford's official last tram, can now be viewed in the city's industrial museum at Moorside Mills. *Geoff Lumb*

Cardiff

Right:
The Welsh capital city had a relatively small and compact standard gauge tramway network that, at its peak, operated over 130 passenger trams across just under 20 route miles. Until the appointment of R. I. Horsfield as General Manager in 1920, it seemed likely that the city's tramways would be a relatively early casualty, but under Horsfield's aegis the tramways were modernised and, in co-operation with Brush, more than 100 new tramcars were built with small diameter wheels so that fully-enclosed trams could operate under the low railway bridges that plagued the system. Two of the resulting Brush-built cars, Nos 56 (in normal fleet livery) and 114 (in wartime khaki), are seen on the Whitchurch Road-St Mary Street route. This route was the last in Cardiff to be converted, succumbing on 19 February 1950. *C. Carter*
(This is the only colour shot of Cardiff known to the author: it is hoped that its rarity will outweigh the slight colour cast.)

Douglas

Right:
The only surviving horse tramway in the British Isles is that of Douglas on the Isle of Man. The first section of the 3ft 0in gauge route was opened in 1876. Douglas Corporation took over in 1902 and, although there were proposals at one time for electrification, 120 years on the trams are still horse-operated. The northern terminus of the single route is at Derby Castle, where the horse trams meet the electric cars of the Manx Electric Railway. With MER No 41 (a trailer built in 1930 following a disastrous fire in April 1930 at the Laxey depot) in the background, one of the Corporation's covered toastracks heads south. *Geoff Lumb*

Dundee

Prewar photographs of trams in colour are scarce, and this example showing the Murraygate in Dundee in May 1937 is of particular interest. The street is decorated for the Coronation of King George VI. Closest to the camera No 18, which dated originally from 1902 but which had been extensively rebuilt, waits as No 4, which dated from 1900 and which had also been substantially altered during its life, uses the crossover. A third tram can be seen heading towards the city centre from the east. The tracks in Murraygate were used for the Maryfield route and were relaid in the early 1950s. The track survived the system's closure and part has been incorporated into a modern pedestrian precinct, reminding locals of their transport history — one of the few tangible remains of Dundee's tramway past.
G. C. Bett/Colour-Rail (IR300)

Although Dundee was perhaps the last of the 'small town' tramways to survive in Britain, its trams were always well-maintained as exemplified by No 54 heading inbound along Lindsay Street with a service from Lochee in August 1953. This particular tram was one of a batch of nine built in the Corporation's own workshops between 1923 and 1925. Originally numbered 91-99, the cars became Nos 77-85 in 1928 and finally Nos 53-56/29-33 in 1936. Nos 53-56 were fitted with EMB Hornless trucks, which had replaced earlier EMB trucks in 1930. The cars were to survive in service until the suspension (and later permanent withdrawal) of the Blackness-Downfield service in November 1955.
Roy Brook

The last cars to be acquired by Dundee Corporation were the 10 Brush-built cars of 1930, Nos 19-28. Wider than the remainder of the fleet, these cars restricted largely to the Lochee route from which they derived their nickname — the 'Lochee' cars. Seen in August 1954 one of the batch, No 25, heads along the High Street *en route* to Lochee. The Lochee route utilised Lindsay Street, Nethergate, High Street and Reform Street to form a city centre terminal loop. The Lochee route and that linking Maryfield with Ninewells were to survive until the final withdrawal of Dundee's trams on 20 October 1956. No 25 was to become the city's last tramcar in service. Although an offer was made to the preservation movement of one of the 'Lochee' cars, the lack of a suitable storage site in the period before the establishment of the National Tramway Museum at Crich meant that the offer had to be declined. None of the 'Lochee' cars was, thus, to survive. *Roy Brook*

The High Street was the centre of tramway operation in Dundee and here we can see, on the right, No 45 preparing to head along the Perth Road towards Ninewells and, on the left, No 55, heading towards Downfield. No 55 was to succumb at the same time as sister car No 54 illustrated earlier, but No 45 was to survive until 1956. The latter car was one of six built by Hurst Nelson in 1920 that were originally numbered 67/68 and 79-82. These cars were built with top covers and were rebuilt as fully enclosed during the modernisation of the Dundee fleet in the early 1930s. *Roy Brook*

Edinburgh

Left:
The bulk of the Edinburgh system was converted to electric traction relatively late, with the majority of routes being operated by cable cars until the early 1920s. Much of the initial electric tram fleet was formed from converted cable cars, but from 1924 onwards a significant number of new electric trams was also delivered. Nos 332-370 were constructed, between 1924 and 1930, in the Corporation's own workshops at Shrubhill as indeed was the majority of the city's tramcar fleet. Typical of this early batch of cars is No 363, which, as one of the later built examples, was delivered fully-enclosed. In the background can be seen No 50, one of the post-1934 cars; this particular example was built in 1950 and inherited the fleet number from one of the last of the converted cable cars to be withdrawn. *Tom Marsh*

Below:
In December 1934 car No 69 emerged as the prototype of the new flush-sided domed-roof cars following on from the experimental No 180 built two years earlier. Between 1934 and 1950, when construction ceased, some 80 of these cars were constructed in Shrubhill Works on Peckham P22 trucks. No 237, built in 1936, is seen operating over the Marchmont Circle route. This route was converted to bus operation on 27 May 1956, some six months before Edinburgh's final conversion. Sister car No 35 was preserved after the final closure. *Tom Marsh*

Fintona

One of the more anachronistic tramway survivors until the 1950s was that of the short horse tramway that linked Fintona proper with Fintona Junction railway station in Ulster. Originally the terminus of a railway line that opened in 1853, Fintona was to be bypassed when the line — later to form part of the Great Northern Railway (Ireland) — was extended to Enniskillen. Thereafter passenger services over the 5ft 3in gauge line were provided by horse-drawn trams.

No 381, illustrated here, was built by the GNR(I) in 1883 and remained in service until the line was to close as part of decimation of the ex-GNR(I) network in Ulster on 30 September 1957. Ironically, the horse tram was to outlive the electric cars in the province. Seen in its blue and white livery, No 381 is pictured departing from Fintona. Following withdrawal, No 381 was preserved. *E. S. Russell/Colour-Rail (IR52)*

Gateshead

The history of Gateshead's tramway network, operated by the Gateshead & District Tramways Co (a subsidiary of British Electric Traction), was inextricably linked with that of its larger neighbour across the Tyne, Newcastle, with which joint services were operated across the river. Although the entire Gateshead system survived until the post-1945 period, conversion of Newcastle's tramway system meant that the future for Gateshead's trams was far from rosy. It was not, however, until 1950 and 1951 that the routes in Gateshead itself were converted, leading to the odd position that Gateshead trams continued to operate into Newcastle a year after the latter's own tramway system had been finally converted. The presence of a number of low railway bridges in the town necessitated the operation of many single-deck cars, such as No 46 seen in Askew Road in March 1951. This was one of a batch of cars built by Milnes, delivered in 1902 and rebuilt in the early 1930s. *I. Davidson/Colour-Rail (IR348)*

Right:
Gateshead also operated a number of double-deck cars, such as No 66 seen with its proud crew at Saltwell Park in March 1951. This was one of a batch of seven cars bought in 1923 and built by Brush. These cars, No 61-67, were the last new trams to be bought by Gateshead; subsequent acquisitions, in 1947 and 1948, were second-hand from Oldham and Newcastle corporations respectively. This photograph must have been taken virtually at the end of operation of the Saltwell Park route, as it was converted to bus operation on 3 March 1951, the first of five abandonments that year which resulted in the final Gateshead tram operating on 4 August. *I. Davidson/Colour-Rail (IR351)*

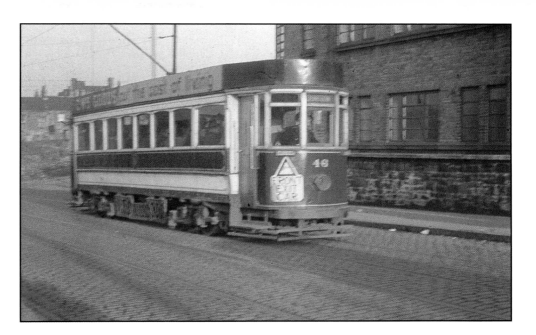

Glasgow

Two generations of Glasgow trams are seen alongside each other during a Light Railway Transport League tour of Glasgow in August 1954. On the left is 'Standard' car No 23, a representative of the largest class of trams to operate outside London. More than 1,000 of the type were built between 1899 and 1924. No 23 was constructed in 1922 and was scrapped in early 1959; sister car No 22 is preserved at the National Tramway Museum. No 1265 was one of the 150 production 'Coronation' type built between 1937 and 1941; this car being completed in October 1939. Originally there were plans for the construction of 600 of this type, but the war intervened. It was the failure to complete this building programme, with the resulting survival of many of the older 'Standard' cars, that undermined the position of Glasgow's system in the 1950s, despite the acquisition of 100 'Cunarders' along with further 'Coronations' and the ex-Liverpool 'Green Goddesses'. *Roy Brook*

Whilst the bulk of the Glasgow fleet was double-deck, a number of single-deck cars were also operated. In 1925 it was decided to construct a high-speed experimental single-deck car to compete with private bus operators over the longer interurban routes, and No 1089 was the result. It was built at the Corporation's Coplawhill Works and was fitted with Brill 77E1 bogies, being completed in 1928. Although successful in electrical terms, No 1089 was not a success operationally due to its lack of seating capacity. As a consequence, it was relegated to the Clydebank-Duntocher service, until that route was converted to bus operation in 1949. After a brief period of storage, the car's seating arrangement was altered and it was then used on workmen's services in Clydebank. Withdrawn again in 1960, the car was again resurrected following the disastrous Dalmarnock depot fire. Final withdrawal came in mid-1961 and the car is now preserved at the Glasgow Museum of Transport. *Roy Brook*

Left:
Following the construction of the 'Standard' four-wheel cars, a class of 50 'Standard' bogie cars (Nos 1091-1140) was built. These cars followed on from two prototype cars, No 142, which was a rebuild of an older 'Standard car' and No 1090, both of which had appeared in 1927. The 50 production cars were completed in 1928 and 1929. Bodies were supplied by Hurst Nelson (50), Brush (10) and R. Y. Pickering (10). The bogies were supplied by the Kilmarnock Engineering Co, and this led to the class's nickname of 'Kilmarnock Bogies'. No 1136, one of the Brush-built examples, is seen crossing the canal bridge at Dalmuir. Services over this bridge were suspended, due to its condition, between 7 September 1959 and 1 August 1960. Route 9, from Dalmuir West to Auchenshuggle, was destined to become Glasgow's last tram route, being converted to bus operation on 4 September 1962. Two of the 'Kilmarnock' Bogies survive, both at the National Tramway Museum: No 1115 in original condition and the much rebuilt No 1100. *Geoff Lumb*

Above:
In 1953 the then Glasgow General Manager, E. R. L. Fitzpayne, reported to his transport committee that Liverpool had offered for sale 20 bogie trams. At this time Glasgow was acutely aware that its fleet of 'Standard' cars was becoming old and urgent replacements were needed. The availability of the 'Green Goddesses' from Liverpool was, therefore, a welcome opportunity and a total of 46 entered service between 1953 and 1956. The cars were modified before entering service, the work including being regauged from 4ft 8½in to 4ft 7¾in. In Glasgow, due to differing clearances, the cars were generally limited to route 29, from Tollcross to Milngavie. The 'Green Goddesses' were to survive for only a few years in Glasgow, being withdrawn between 1957 and 1960. One of the cars, No 1055, was to be preserved and can now be seen at the National Tramway Museum in its original Liverpool condition. *Tom Marsh*

Great Orme

Although the 3ft 6in gauge Great Orme Tramway possessed overhead until recently, it is not an electric tramway. Nor, despite the cable between the running lines, is it a cable tramway. It is, rather, a long funicular, where the ascending car is assisted by the descent of its twin. The line, which opened in 1902 and 1903, is in two sections, which meet, appropriately, at Halfway. Each section is provided with two cars, all four of which were built by Hurst Nelson. Cars Nos 4 and 5 serve the lower section, whilst Nos 6 and 7 serve the upper. In total the two sections are just about a mile in length, with the average gradient on the lower section being 1 in 6.5 and that on the upper being 1 in 15.5. No 4 is seen preparing to depart from Halfway on 11 June 1962.
Geoff Lumb

Grimsby & Immingham

Built originally by the Great Central Railway, the Grimsby & Immingham passed via the LNER to British Railways in 1948. One of the consequences of the Nationalisation of the line was that its fleet of cars was repainted after 1951 in the standard BR green livery for electrified stock. Although the short street section at the Grimsby end, between Cleveland Bridge and Corporation Bridge, was threatened with closure in the late 1940s, this section did not finally close until 1956. Car No 4, one of the original ex-GCR cars dating from 1911, heads back towards Grimsby along the Humber estuary. At 54ft 2in in length, these were the longest first-generation single-deck trams to operate in Britain. The remaining section of the Grimsby & Immingham finally succumbed, after the long drawn out closure procedure, on 1 July 1961; No 4 was destined to be the official last car. Sister car No 14 is preserved. *Geoff Lumb*

As part of its re-equipment programme for the line British Railways acquired three ex-Newcastle cars in 1948 and 19 cars from Gateshead in 1951. Of the Gateshead cars, 17 entered service and one became a works' car. The 19th car was destroyed in an accident whilst it was being unloaded. Three of the ex-Gateshead cars, Nos 17, 26 and 22, are seen at the line's Pyewipe depot on 18 April 1960. These were originally Gateshead Nos 57, 10 and 7 and were built between 1921 and 1928. All three were constructed in Gateshead's own workshops. On the closure of the line, No 10 was to be preserved and can now be seen at the National Tramway Museum. Sister car No 5 is on display at the North of England Open Air Museum at Beamish. *Geoff Lumb*

Hill of Howth

The longest-surviving tramway in the Republic of Ireland was the ex-Great Northern Railway of Ireland's line that served the rocky Howth promontory to the northeast of Dublin. The line linked the GNR(I) stations of Howth and Sutton. Constructed to the 5ft 3in gauge, the line opened in two stages during 1901. In 1953, following a period of increasing financial strain, the GNR(I), including the tramway, was taken into the ownership of the governments in both the Republic and Ulster.

Notices announcing the tramway's closure appeared in January 1954, but the line was reprieved until final closure came on 31 March 1959. To operate the line, eight Brush built cars, Nos 1-8, were delivered in 1901; these were supplemented by two additional passenger cars in 1902. There was also a single works car. Seen in the line's blue and white livery, No 5 is pictured at St Finyans. Although this car was scrapped on closure, sister cars Nos 2 and 4 do survive in preservation. *Roy Brook*

Leeds

Left:

In 1931/32 Leeds Corporation placed in service 100 four-wheel trams, Nos 155-254, built to the design of the then General Manager, R. L. Horsfield, by Brush. These 100 cars, which became known as 'Showboats' or 'Horsfields', followed on from four earlier prototype cars, Nos 151-154, which had been built at Kirkstall Works. The first 50 were fitted with BTH equipment and the remainder with equipment supplied by GEC. One of the latter, No 249, is seen at the terminus of the Meanwood route in early 1955. The Meanwood route was converted to bus operation on 25 June 1955. The GEC-fitted cars were destined to be withdrawn earlier than those fitted with BTH equipment, and No 249 was one of a number of the type to be scrapped at Low Fields Road yard in 1956. *Roy Brook*

Below:

As a result of the gradual conversion of London's remaining tram routes, the capital's 'Feltham' cars were offered for sale. Leeds had taken LPTB No 2099 on loan in September 1949 to test the type's suitability and acquired a further 89 in 1950/51, although not all were destined to enter service. No 2099 was renumbered 501 in Leeds and the remainder of the type became Nos 502-90. No 525, originally LPTB No 2083 and Metropolitan Electric Tramways No 339, is seen in 1955. This particular car was one of many of the ex-MET cars to survive until the end of tramway operation in Leeds, on 7 November 1959; the ex-London United Tramways batch, Nos 551-590, were less successful and, except for those that had had their equipment replaced, were withdrawn earlier. Like the 'Horsfields', it was the GEC-fitted cars that succumbed earlier due to problems in obtaining spares. *Roy Brook*

As part of its proposals for postwar reconstruction, Leeds Corporation unveiled plans for the construction of city centre tram subways, but these were in the event to come to nought. However, in furtherance of the scheme three single-deck cars were constructed. The first of these numerically, No 600, was built at Kirkstall Works between 1949 and 1953. The car had been originally Sunderland No 85 and had been sold to Leeds in 1944. It was never operated by Leeds in its original condition, although it was renumbered 288 in 1948 prior to its rebuilding. With the failure to construct the subways, No 600 eked out its existence until it was withdrawn in 1957. The car is seen here at Thwaite Gate in August 1954. It was preserved and can now be seen at the National Tramway Museum. *Roy Brook*

In 1951 the Transport Department was authorised to construct two single-deck cars and the local firm of Charles H. Roe won the contract. These two cars, Nos 601 and 602, were destined to be the only trams built by the company. The two cars were delivered in 1953 and were painted in a striking purple and cream livery to mark the Coronation of HM Queen Elizabeth II. However, by this date, the local Labour Party had decided on a policy of tramway abandonment — a policy which it was able to carry through when it gained control of the Council in May 1953. Although No 601 was relatively traditional, No 602, with its all-electric control system, was perhaps the most modern first-generation tramcar to operate in Britain. As with No 600, the car was never to fulfil its potential and spent much of its time operating the short Hunslet route. It is pictured here in August 1954 at New Inn. It was withdrawn in 1957 and can also be seen at Crich. Sister car No 601 was also preserved, at the Middleton Railway, but it was later dismantled. *Roy Brook*

Liverpool

The City of Liverpool possessed one of the most innovative and modern tramway networks in Britain. Throughout the 1920s the system received new tramcars and several extensions were constructed, the majority of the latter being on reserved track. In 1932 the Corporation confirmed that the tram was to remain the cornerstone of future public transport development in the city and the scene was set for further radical change over the next decade. Although the majority of enthusiasts recall the two designs of streamline car that emerged from the mid-1930s, prior to the introduction of these trams Liverpool Corporation constructed a number of non-streamlined cars in its own workshops. However, by the later 1940s the tide had turned against the tramcar in Liverpool, as elsewhere, and the process of conversion had commenced. *C. Carter*

As in Blackpool, an inspirational General Manager, Walter Marks, was to play an important role in the modernisation of Liverpool's tramway network. From the mid-1930s through until the early years of World War 2 more than 250 streamlined trams and numerous extensions were constructed, providing the city with a network that was second to none in Great Britain. The most numerous of the Liverpool 'Streamliners' were the bogie 'Green Goddesses'. The first of these entered service in 1936 and by the end of the following year more than 160 had been built in the Corporation's own Edge Lane Works. The cars were fitted with a variety of bogies and electrical equipment. No 968, illustrated here on route 19 to Kirkby in August 1954, was fitted with EMB 'Heavyweight' bogies and GEC WT184A motors. This particular car was withdrawn in early 1956. Service 19 was to survive longer, being converted to bus operation in November the same year. Although 46 'Green Goddesses' were to migrate northwards to Glasgow, No 968 was not amongst them and like all those that remained in Liverpool was scrapped. The only 'Green Goddess' to survive is No 869, which was preserved following withdrawal in Glasgow. *Roy Brook*

Also seen on route 19 is streamlined four-wheel car No 214. The type, known as 'Baby Grands', was developed alongside the 'Green Goddesses', although the first of the type, No 201, did not appear until 26 November 1937. Between then and October 1942 (when the last of the type entered service) a total of 100 were built, again Edge Lane Works being the builder. EMB won the contract to supply the trucks; the first 13 (Nos 201-213) received Metro-Vick motors, whilst the remainder were fitted with BTH motors. The 'Baby Grands' were to outlast the 'Green Goddesses' in service, and some 30 remained operational at the final closure on 14 September 1957. Thirteen cars, including No 214, appeared in the closure procession; sister car No 293 was painted in a reversed livery of white with green lining as Liverpool's official last tram. Two of the 'Baby Grands', Nos 245 and 293, survive. *Tom Marsh*

Below:
Two of the 'Baby Grand' four-wheelers are pictured close to the Mersey Tunnel entrance in August 1954. No 211 was fitted with Metro-Vick motors, whilst No 285 had BTH motors. Service 13, from the Pier Head to Lower Lane, was converted to bus operation in November 1955, whilst the 6A, from the Pier Head to Bowring Park, was to survive to become one of the last two Liverpool routes, being converted on 14 September 1957. All the Liverpool streamlined cars had a propensity to burst into flames, and No 211 was stored during 1956 having succumbed to a small fire in the resistance cupboard; it was not to operate again. No 285 was scrapped at Edge Lane Works in October 1956. *Roy Brook*

Llandudno & Colwyn Bay

Below:

The Llandudno & Colwyn Bay Electric Railway was a 3ft 6in gauge electric tramway that linked the two North Wales coastal resorts of its title. Its small fleet of attractively-liveried trams served the community for almost 50 years and, when threatened with closure in the mid-1950s, there was a determined effort to preserve the line. Unfortunately, these efforts came to nothing and the line was to be replaced with buses on 24 March 1956. In 1932/33 the L&CBER acquired five single-deck cars from Accrington. These cars, which were originally 4ft 0in in gauge, dated from 1920 and were built by Brush. No 4, illustrated here, was one of three of the batch to receive bogies from the original L&CBER trams. *Tom Marsh*

Right:

Further second-hand trams, in the guise of 10 open-top double-deckers from Bournemouth, came to North Wales during 1936. Numbered 6-15, these cars had originally been built in 1914 (No 6) and 1921-26 (the remainder). No 8, which had been Bournemouth No 116, is seen at the Little Orme Cafe in August 1954. Following the closure of the L&CBER, No 6 was preserved. It is currently displayed in Bournemouth having been restored to its original Bournemouth condition as No 85. *Roy Brook*

Left:
Four open toastrack trams, Nos 19-22, were delivered to the L&CBER in 1920. They were built by English Electric and were fitted with English Electric bogies. The first of the quartet, No 19, is pictured heading towards Llandudno on a day when, no doubt, the passengers were enjoying the open nature of the car. Note the somewhat precipitous position adopted by the conductor; no doubt, today's Health & Safety Executive would have made a comment about this type of operation! *Tom Marsh*

Above:
Much of the L&CBER was constructed using sleeper track over private rights of way. One such section was that at Penrhynside and here we see ex-Bournemouth car No 14 (Bournemouth No 121) heading north up the gradient *en route* to Llandudno. This car, along with all the other ex-Bournemouth trams (with the exception of the older No 6), was built by Brush and was fitted with Brill 22E bogies. *Tom Marsh*

London

Coming under unified control only in 1933, with the creation of the London Passenger Transport Board, London possessed Britain's biggest tramway network and, in the 'E/1s', the largest single class of trams to operate anywhere in the country. A total of some 1,050 were built for the London County Council between 1907 and 1930. No 1273, seen here operating on route 40 between Woolwich and Savoy Street, was one of 200 built by Hurst Nelson in 1910. This route was of those that survived through until the final part, Stage 8, of 'Operation Tramaway', on 5/6 July 1952. Two of the 'E1/s' survive in preservation — No 1025 at the London Transport Museum and No 1622 which is currently being restored as a 'Rehab' car for operation at the National Tramway Museum. *C. Carter*

Right:
Along with the LCC, a number of municipal operators were also taken over by the LPTB. These included Walthamstow, West Ham, East Ham and Croydon. In 1933 the LPTB inherited a fleet of some 62 cars from Walthamstow Corporation and, although the routes over which the cars originally operated were converted to trolleybus operation during the 1930s, 20 were to survive until 1952 having been transferred to the south London routes. No 2050 is seen operating on route 72 from Savoy Street to Woolwich, which was another of those services to survive until July 1952. No 2050 (Walthamstow No 59) was one of a batch of 12 cars (Nos 2042-53) delivered in 1927 that were similar in design to the LCC's 'E/1s'. They were built by Hurst Nelson and were fitted with Heenan & Froude maximum traction bogies. *C. Carter*

Left:
Three companies — the Metropolitan Electric Tramways, the London United Tramways and the South Metropolitan Electric Tramways — also became part of the LPTB in 1933. In the late 1920s MET and LUT had been involved in the development of a replacement type of double-deck tram, which became known as the 'Feltham'. A total of 100 of the production cars were manufactured, with 54 going to MET and 46 to LUT. Again, although the routes over which they were designed to operate were converted to trolleybus operation during the 1930s, the 'Felthams' were to survive until 1950/51 through being transferred to the south London routes. No 2151, originally LUT No 382, is seen about to depart on a working to Tooting Broadway on route 10. This route was converted to bus operation on 6/7 January 1951 and three months later No 2151 was withdrawn. The car was then transferred to Leeds (as No 576) before being finally withdrawn for scrap in July 1956. None of the ex-LUT 'Felthams' survive, although two of the ex-MET cars do — No 2085 in the USA and No 2099 in the London Transport Museum. *C. Carter*

In 1932, just prior to the creation of the LPTB, the LCC built experimental car No 1, which, it was hoped, would form the basis of the new standard class for operation in the Metropolis. Nicknamed 'Bluebird', because of its non-standard original blue livery, No 1 was built at Charlton Works and fitted with EMB heavyweight equal-wheel bogies. It was, however, destined to remain unique as the LPTB decided on a policy of tramcar replacement. Despite being non-standard, No 1 was to survive in service until 1951 when it was sold to Leeds as part of the contract for the 'Felthams' as a replacement for two cars destroyed before delivery to the Yorkshire city. As No 301 it ran for a further six years until withdrawal in 1957. It was subsequently preserved and can now be seen at Crich. *Tom Marsh*

Although it was apparent shortly after the end of World War 2 that tram conversion (to bus rather than trolleybus) was to remain the avowed policy of both the LPTB and its successor the London Transport Executive, it was not until 1950 that resources were available to enable 'Operation Tramaway' to start. Over the next two years, London's remaining 800 trams were gradually replaced, culminating with the final stage on 5/6 July 1952. Wearing the chalked farewell slogans that 'graced' many of the London trams is 'E/3' class No 1931. The 100 'E/3s'. Nos 1904-2003, were built by the LCC in 1930/31 and sister car No 1951 was destined to become London's last tram — a journey poignantly recalled in the classic film *The Elephant Will Never Forget*. Unfortunately, none of the 'E/3s' survived into preservation. *Tom Marsh*

Manx Electric Railway

At 17 miles in length the Manx Electric Railway is the longest of all the surviving 'traditional' tramways. Constructed to the 3ft 0in gauge, the line, which links Douglas with Ramsey, runs up the east coast of the Isle of Man. The line opened in two stages, from Douglas to Laxey in 1893 and thence to Ramsey the following year. Although there have been threats of closure, including the suspension of services north from Laxey between 1975 and 1977, the line survives and, with it, a collection of trams that are amongst the oldest in operation worldwide. No 19, a fully-enclosed car built by Milnes in 1899, hauls an unidentified toastrack trailer south at Groudle Glen curve in 1956. *Roy Brook*

Rotherham

Although the bulk of the Rotherham tramway system had succumbed to trolleybus and motorbus operation by the early 1930s, the unwillingness of Sheffield Corporation to convert the joint Rotherham-Sheffield route meant that Rotherham was forced to maintain the operation of this single route. In order to maintain the service, 11 new trams, built by English Electric, were delivered in 1934/35. These trams were unusual in that they were single-ended, owing much in their design to contemporary trolleybuses. To facilitate short workings at the borough boundary at Templeborough a reversing stub was installed. No 10 is pictured towards the end of its working life. The through services between Sheffield and Rotherham were suspended in 1948 to allow for bridge repairs, but were never reinstated. Rotherham's final trams ran on 13 November 1949. None of the single-ended cars were to survive. *C. Carter*

Sheffield

The city of Sheffield was the last major operator in England to bid farewell to the trams, when the final routes were converted to bus operation on 8 October 1960. At the start of the 1950s Sheffield, with its fleet of blue and cream four-wheel trams, was widely regarded as one of the most secure of all tramway operators, but despite considerable opposition, tramway abandonment became official policy in 1951. One of Brush-built cars of 1926/27, No 44, is seen at Wadsley Bridge in July 1953 with a service for Woodseats. The Woodseats-Wadsley Bridge service was converted to bus operation on 3 October 1959. Note the unusual banjo-shaped extension to the driver's windscreen; this was to allow the brake handle to be easily rotated. *Roy Brook*

Also fitted with the banjo-shaped lower windscreen is Cravens-built No 478, which was one of a batch of 50, Nos 451-500, delivered in 1926/27. The tram is seen at the Handsworth terminus in July 1953, some four years before this route was converted to bus operation. These trams were the last to be delivered to Sheffield with a rocker panel; thereafter all Sheffield's new trams (with the exception of the second-hand acquisitions from Newcastle and Bradford) had flush side panels. The final withdrawal of the rocker panel cars, in 1957, was marked by a series of tours. Only part of one of the Cravens-built trams survives — the lower deck of No 460 in the Sheffield Transport Museum. *Roy Brook*

Typical of the flush-sided 'Standard' cars built between 1928 and 1936 is No 217, which is seen at the terminus of the Prince of Wales route shortly after the conversion of the Intake route on 6 October 1956. Some 210 cars of this type were built, the majority by the Corporation at Queen's Road, with 25 (Nos 131-155) being built by W. & E. Hill Ltd; all were fitted with Peckham P22 trucks. The Prince of Wales route was to be converted to bus operation on 12 April 1958. One of the 'Standards', No 189, is preserved at the National Tramway Museum.
Roy Brook

During World War 2, 14 trams were destroyed as the result of enemy action in an air raid on 12 December 1940. Between 1941 and 1944 replacement cars, using the same fleet numbers, were constructed. These replacement cars were built to the improved 'Standard' — or 'Domed Roof' — type that had been introduced in 1936. Again all were fitted with Peckham P22 trucks. Of the 14, 12 were older 'Standard' cars, and one of these 12, No 112, is pictured. The routes from Millhouses and Beauchief to Weedon Street and Vulcan Road were the last Sheffield routes to be converted. *Geoff Lumb*

Left:
In 1946 the Corporation unveiled its first new postwar double-deck tram, No 501, and in 1948 authorisation was gained for the construction of 35 new cars. The contract went to the Horbury-based company of Charles Roberts & Co — that company's first foray into tramcar building. The first of the production trams, No 502, entered service in May 1950, and the remainder followed suit over the next two years; the last, No 536, appearing in April 1952. However, by that date the Corporation had decided on a conversion programme and the 'Roberts' cars were destined to have a relatively short life. Here No 506 uses the trolley reverser at Beauchief. Until 28 February 1959 the tracks extended beyond this point to provide a link with Woodseats. *Geoff Lumb*

Right:
Representatives of two of Sheffield's last types of tramcar, headed by 'Roberts' No 528, are seen at Vulcan Road in June 1960, some four months before the system finally closed. Vulcan Road was adjacent to the tram depot at Tinsley, from where most of Sheffield's trams made the one-way journey to the local scrapyard of T. W. Ward. Two of the 'Roberts' cars, Nos 510 and 513, received special liveries to mark the system's closure and both were preserved: No 510 at the National Tramway Museum and No 513 at Beamish. Also preserved is one of the 'Domed Roof' cars, No 264, which can also be seen at Crich. *Roy Brook*

Snaefell Mountain Railway

Snaefell Mountain Railway, which opened in 1895, provides a link from Laxey up to the summit of Snaefell, which, at 2,100ft, is the highest peak on the Isle of Man. Built to the 3ft 6in gauge, rather than the Manx standard gauge of 3ft 0in, in order to accommodate the Fell third rail, the SMR continues in operation to this day. In May 1960 two of the SMR's fleet of six trams, Nos 2 (in the short-lived green livery) and 6 (in the more traditional brown, red and white livery), can be seen at the Laxey terminus. *Roy Brook*

Pictured in May 1960, SMR No 3 is one of the six cars that were supplied to operate the line in 1895 by Milnes. Just visible at the front of the nearest bogie are the pincers that form an integral part of the Fell patent brake.

Of the six cars built in 1895, five remain in service in the centenary year; the sixth, No 5, was rebuilt in 1971 following the original car's destruction by fire. *Roy Brook*

Southampton

Right:
Although the Southampton network had
survived the ravages of World War 2
relatively well, the condition of both the
vehicles and the track was such that it came
as no surprise that abandonment soon
became official policy. The town's fully-
enclosed double-deck trams had a peculiar
roof profile, the result of operation through
the famous Bargate with its restricted height.
The Bargate was bypassed during the 1930s,
when the demolition of adjacent buildings
allowed the tram tracks to be diverted around
it. The profile of the roof is shown to good
advantage in this view of one of the town's
four-wheel cars. The last Southampton trams
operated on 31 December 1949, although a
number migrated north to Leeds where they
gave a few years of further service. *C. Carter*

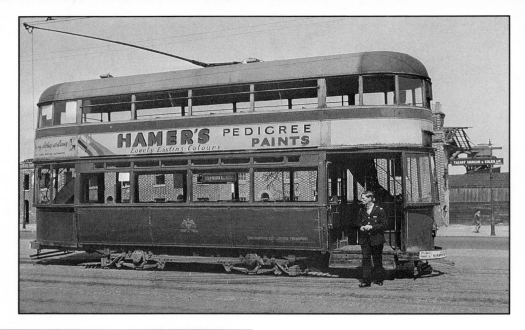

Left:
Pictured in October 1949, two months before
the system's final closure, No 8 heads for the
Floating Bridge terminus along Shirley Road.
This car was built in the Corporation's own
workshops in the early 1920s and was fitted
with a Peckham P35 truck. On withdrawal,
the car, along with others, was sold to Leeds
Corporation. However, No 8 was destined
never to reach Leeds and was ultimately
scrapped on the South Coast. Other cars did
enter service in Leeds, although the
acquisition of the ex-London 'Feltham' cars
and the decision to convert the Leeds system
to bus operation meant that the ex-
Southampton cars had a relatively short life
in Yorkshire, all being withdrawn by 1953.
Similar vintage No 11 has been preserved
after years of dereliction and is currently
being restored. *W. E. Robertson/Colour-Rail
(IR368)*

Sunderland

In 1938, two years before the final abandonment of Huddersfield's system, Sunderland acquired the eight English Electric-built cars of 1931/32 that had been the final trams delivered to the West Riding operator. Regauged from 4ft 7³/₄in to 4ft 8¹/₂in, the cars were to survive in the northeast until the final run-down of the Sunderland system. No 33, seen here running along the Durham Road route on 9 May 1953, was originally Huddersfield No 141. The Durham Road route was extended in two stages during the late 1940s, making it one of the relatively few postwar tramway extensions in Britain; it was, however, to have a very short life, being converted to bus operation on 28 March 1954.
D. Charlton/Colour-Rail

By April 1954 the Sunderland network had been reduced to a single route which ran north from the town, past the depot at Fulwell, to the coast at Seaburn. Heading southwards on 19 April that year is No 95, which is caught passing the dramatic station building at Monkwearmouth. This building still survives and now forms the home of the local railway museum. No 95 was one of a batch of nine cars built by English Electric and fitted with EMB Hornless trucks that were delivered in 1933.
The late Eric Russell/Colour-Rail

Also delivered in 1933 were five double-deck cars (Nos 21, 24, 96-98), also fitted with EMB Hornless trucks, that were manufactured in Sunderland's own workshops. No 96 is pictured at the Library on 19 April 1954. The Seaburn route, the last to operate in Sunderland, was converted to bus operation on 1 October 1954. Of the town's remarkable collection of trams, which boasted second-hand examples from Accrington, Portsmouth, South Shields and London, as well as the aforementioned Huddersfield cars, only one was to be preserved on withdrawal — the unique prototype 'Feltham' car that is now on display at the National Tramway Museum. *The late Eric Russell/Colour-Rail*

Swansea & Mumbles

The Brush-built cars for the Swansea & Mumbles were the largest of all British first generation tramcars and seated a total of 106 — 48 on the lower deck and 58 on the upper. The trams were also fitted for multiple operation, and pairs were often run. Unusually, the trams only had entrances on one — the landward — side. The Swansea & Mumbles was almost six miles in length, being served by eight intermediate stops. Due to the complexity of the line's legal position, its operators, the South Wales Transport Co (a subsidiary of British Electric Traction), had to obtain a private Act of Parliament to facilitate closure. Pictured in July 1955 No 5 is pictured near Swansea Bay.
T. J. Edginton/Colour-Rail (IR122)

Volks Railway

Although Blackpool can lay claim to being the first electric tramway in Britain, two years earlier, in 1883, Magnus Volk had inaugurated the first public electric railway in Britain. The original line, of 2ft gauge ran for a quarter of a mile along the Brighton sea front. Power was gained from one of the running rails. At the end of the 1883 season the line was closed and regauged to 2ft 9in and a third rail installed. In the 20th century the line was again regauged, this time to 2ft 8½in. The line has also been extended and now runs for 1¼ miles from the Marina to the Aquarium. A fleet of nine cars, the oldest dating from 1892, continues to operate over the mainly single-track route. There are three stations and two passing loops. Two of the line's cars are seen passing on 27 June 1993.
Peter Waller

Preservation

Bradford

The West Yorkshire Transport Museum project dates back to the early 1980s. This ambitious scheme foresaw the creation of an integrated transport museum on derelict railway land at Low Moor, south of Bradford, linked to the reopening of the Spen Valley line through Cleckheaton as an electric tramway. Unfortunately, these proposals were to be undermined by the abolition of the West Yorkshire Metropolitan County Council in April 1986. The project, however, survived and as 'Transperience' a modified scheme opened in mid-1995. In order to operate the tramway, the museum gathered together a number of tramcars from Britain and overseas. Subsequently a number of these have been disposed of, but two that remain are four-wheel cars that came from Budapest — Nos 2576/2577. The former is seen on 2 November 1986 being shunted at the museum's temporary store (the now demolished former BR DMU depot at Hammerton Street) by one of the collection's industrial locomotives on the occasion of the formal acceptance of the ex-Budapest cars into the collection. Nos 2576/2577, now fully restored, provide the tram service at 'Transperience'. *Peter Waller*

Birkenhead

It was in Birkenhead that the history of the tramcar in Britain started, as it was in this town that the American George Francis Train inaugurated his first horse tramway in the country on 30 August 1860. More than 130 years later Birkenhead can lay claim to another first, with the opening of the first heritage tramway to feature street running. Such heritage tramways, which have proved very popular elsewhere, most notably in the United States of America, had not appeared in Britain until the opening, in early 1995, of the short Birkenhead route. To operate the route two trams were constructed in Hong Kong — very similar in style to the colony's own electric tramcars — numbered 69 and 70. The numbers were selected because Birkenhead's first-generation tramway, which was finally abandoned in July 1937, reached fleet number 68. One of the two cars is seen on 29 May 1995 alongside preserved ex-Douglas horse tram No 46 (a Milnes Voss-built car withdrawn in 1987) and a recently restored ex-Birkenhead Corporation open-top double-deck car. *Paul Collins*

Black Country Museum

Right:
Situated near Dudley, in the West Midlands, the Black Country Museum has a short 3ft 6in gauge line. Currently, the only operational car is Dudley, Stourbridge & District single-deck car No 5, which is seen here on 24 May 1987. The car was originally built at the company's Tividale Works in 1920. At the time of writing, a double-deck tram and a second single-deck car are nearing completion and it is hoped that these additional cars will be in service shortly.
Peter Waller

Carlton Colville

Left:
Now established for more than quarter of a century, the East Anglian Transport Museum at Carlton Colville has a fascinating collection of road vehicles both from Britain and from Europe. It is one of only a handful of museums in Britain where it is possible to see both trams and trolleybuses in operation side-by-side. Amongst the museum's operational fleet of tramcars is Blackpool 'Standard' No 159, which is seen at the museum on 16 July 1995. No 159 was one of two 'Standards' to be converted for use as illuminated cars in Blackpool in 1959; it operated alongside sister car No 158 until withdrawal in 1966. No 158 passed to the National Tramway Museum, where it was dismantled for spares. Other operational trams at Carlton Colville include the only surviving London 'HR/2' and a single-deck four-wheel car from Amsterdam. *Peter Waller*

Crich

The National Tramway Museum has now been established in Derbyshire for more than 35 years and has been operating electric trams for three decades. It is a sobering fact that the Museum has now been operational for longer than many of the tramway systems from which its exhibits are derived. The Museum has also achieved an enviable reputation for the quality of its vehicle restoration, both on site and, as in the case of London County Council No 106, elsewhere. This 'B' type car was originally built in 1903 and converted, along with others of the type, into a snowbroom in the late 1920s, becoming No 022. The conversion involved the complete removal of the upper deck and staircases along with modification to the underframes. As such the car was to survive until the conversion of London's trams when it was scheduled for preservation at the Museum of British Transport in Clapham. In 1971 the car was transferred to the Tramway Museum Society and restoration commenced. It was transferred to Crich in early 1983. It is seen here, in September 1985 in fully restored condition — a tribute to the team that undertook its restoration.
Michael H. Waller

Heaton Park

After the closure of the Manchester route that served it, the terminal stub in Heaton Park was covered over and remained undisturbed for 50 years. However, uncovered and now extended into the park proper, the track again resounds with the noise of electric trams. In 1985, when one of the tramway's own vehicles was on temporary loan to Blackpool for that town's tramway centenary celebrations, 'Boat' No 600 was loaned to Heaton Park; it has subsequently returned to Manchester on long-term loan. It is seen here, on 12 June 1988 at the gates to the park. *Peter Waller*

Seaton

Shortly after World War 2 the late Claude Lane constructed a number of miniature trams which proved to be popular both as an attraction at fairs and, later, at various coastal resorts. This led to the construction of a more permanent line at Eastbourne from the mid-1950s. Following the closure of the ex-London & South Western branch line to Seaton in 1966 allied with the approaching end of the lease at Eastbourne, it was decided to transfer operations to the Devon coast and construction of the 2ft 9in gauge line — the gauge had been 2ft 0in at Eastbourne — commenced in early 1970. Passenger services were inaugurated in April 1971 and the line has been gradually extended so that it now runs from close to the seafront in Seaton, up the old railway to a terminus at Colyton. Over the years an impressive collection of trams, some of them incorporating parts from older vehicles, has been built up, exemplified by No 16 seen here at the Colyton terminus.
Peter Durham

75

Second Generation Systems

Tyne & Wear Metro

Based around the former electrified suburban railway lines linking Newcastle with the coast at Tynemouth, the Tyne & Wear Metro commenced operation in 1980. More heavy than light rail, a fleet of 90 articulated vehicles, Nos 4001-90, built by Metro-Cammell in Birmingham, is in operation.

Since the first section opened the network has been progressively extended, with the most recent section to be completed being that to Newcastle Airport which opened in 1991. Seen in Tyne & Wear's yellow and white livery, No 4026 nears Heworth with a St James to Pelaw service. *Brian Morrison*

Docklands Light Railway

In the early 1980s it became apparent that without improved transport links the government's proposals for the regeneration of London's declining docklands area would fail. A variety of options were examined, culminating in the construction of the first stage of the Docklands Light Railway from Tower Gateway to Island Gardens or Stratford. Such was the success of this first phase, following its opening in 1987 that further extensions were authorised. An underground link to Bank was completed and, in 1994, an eastwards extension to Beckton was opened. Further proposals envisage an extension south of the Thames through Greenwich to Lewisham. Heart of the DLR system is the major junction at Poplar and two of the P89 cars, built by BREL in 1989, Nos 19 and 21, are seen at Poplar between West Ferry and West India Quay stations. *Brian Morrison*

Manchester Metrolink

The Manchester Metrolink project was the first second-generation electric tramway in Britain that featured at its core street running. The first section, utilising the old British Rail lines north from Victoria to Bury and south from Piccadilly to Altrincham linked by street running through central Manchester, opened in stages during 1992. At Piccadilly station, Metrolink is served by low-level platforms underneath the main line station. In this view one of the system's Italian-built articulated cars ascends from Piccadilly *en route* to Altrincham on 13 May 1995. *Peter Waller*

South Yorkshire Supertram

Right:
The second of the new-generation electric tramways to open was the South Yorkshire Supertram, which was officially opened by HRH The Princess Royal on 23 May 1994. The current network forms a reverse 'y', with Halfway in the south, being linked to Middlewood and Meadowhall in the north via Sheffield city centre. Unlike Manchester Metrolink, which inherited two former BR heavy rail routes, the Supertram is much more like a traditional street tramway, with considerable lengths of track shared with other road users. The fleet of trams to operate the network was constructed by Siemens-Duewag in Germany. Each articulated car is some 35m in length and provides accommodation for 88 seated passengers as well as numerous standing places. Car No 24 is pictured on 4 August 1995 whilst heading towards Halfway past Sheffield Cathedral.
Paul Collins

Back cover:
Although the Swansea & Mumbles could lay claim to being the oldest passenger-carrying line in the world, with a history that stretched right back to the first decade of the 19th century, for tramway historians it also has another claim to fame — it was the last wholly-new first generation electric tramway to open. Electric services were only inaugurated on 2 March 1929 when a fleet of 13 Brush-built double-deck cars entered service. One of the cars, No 2, is seen at Mumbles Pier in 1959 shortly before the line between Southend and Mumbles was abandoned to allow for the conversion of the route to bus operation. The Swansea & Mumbles trams last operated on 5 January 1960. Although No 2 survived for a period in preservation, following vandalism it was subsequently dismantled. A cab from another car does, however, survive in Swansea. *Roy Brook*

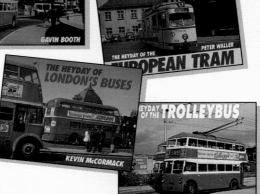